York Rite Freemason's Handbook

JAMES F. HATCHER III

ISBN-13: 978-1505249262
ISBN-10: 1505249260

Available from Amazon.com, CreateSpace.com,
and other retail outlets

www.CreateSpace.com/5134508

Published by The Masonic Press.
Find more related titles on our website:

masonicpress.com

Printed by CreateSpace, Charleston, SC
An Amazon.com Company

THIS BOOK BELONGS TO

_____

NAME

_____

CHAPTER   NO.

_____

COUNCIL   NO.

_____

COMMANDERY   NO.

_____

PHONE

_____

EMAIL

**IF FOUND, PLEASE CONTACT THE OWNER
AND ARRANGE FOR THE RETURN OF
THIS VERY PERSONAL RECORD BOOK.**

YOUR MARK

DEDICATION

This book is dedicated to all of those Freemasons, who, year after year, decade after decade, century after century, have and will continue to strive to help others and work hard to make the world we live in a better place for those of our future generations.

I
have
visited the
Sacred Sanctuary
and have seen the glory

of the Temple.

TABLE OF CONTENTS

ACKNOWLEDGMENTS

Special thanks goes out the York Rite Bodies of North America for selected text, and to Bro. Jeff Day at kingsolomonslodge.org for the use of selected Masonic logo graphics.

YORK RITE
OF
FREEMASONRY

1 ROYAL ARCH MASONRY

Rummaging among the very old records of the Order in the mid-1700s, York Mason first discovered the Royal Arch Degree, which had probably lain dormant for centuries; during which time, it would appear, the society had been confined almost exclusively to operative masons; who continued the ceremonies only of the apprentice, fellow-craft, and master mason, these being deemed appropriate to their occupation.

Founded in 1797, in Boston, Massachusetts, as a national organization, the General Grand Chapter, Royal Arch Masons, International now has jurisdiction over half the 7,000 Chapters in the world, including several provinces in Canada, the Grand Chapters of USA, Philippines, Germany, Italy, Spain, Portugal, and many chapters in Central and South America. Upon your exaltation as a Royal Arch Mason you will become a member of the oldest and largest rite of Royal Arch Masonry.

One of the most fascinating aspects of Royal Arch Masonry has always been how so many men, from so many different walks of life, can meet together in peace, never have any political or religious debates, always conduct their affairs in harmony and friendship, and call each other brother.

No Rite of Freemasonry covers the world so much as does Royal

Arch Masonry. In every country of the earth, on every continent and on many isles of the sea, Will be found Royal Arch Chapters, eager and willing to receive their companions from other parts of the world into that full fellowship that characterizes Royal Arch Masonry.

All Royal Arch Masons believe in one God and in respect for each other. Royal Arch Masonry contains some simple, plain statements of Truth, easily understandable and helpful in our relation to life. Lodge symbolism deals with lessons of the material side of life. The Chapter degrees, and particularly the Royal Arch, deal with the spiritual side of life. Upon your exaltation as a Royal Arch Mason you will become a member of the oldest and largest rite of Freemasonry.

Qualifications

Royal Arch Masonry is the logical step for every Master Mason to take. If after becoming a Royal Arch Mason, you desire to continue your studies, you may take the Council Degrees and the Commandery Orders, both of which are illustrative of and carry forward the principles of the Royal Arch. Any Royal Arch Macon will eagerly propose your name as a candidate for the advancement in the mysteries of Freemasonry. Anyone seeking Membership in the Royal Arch must sign a Petition, stating his age, occupation and place of residence. Members of the Chapter vote by ballot. To be accepted, the ballot must be unanimous.

What has attracted so many Brethren to seek further light in Royal Arch Masonry? The Royal Arch Degrees was considered most important in the early years of Freemasonry and so dogmatic was the Mother Grand Lodge - from which all Speculative Masonry derives - that in 1813, when the two grand lodges in England united, a firm and solemn landmark was adopted and placed in the Articles of Union to guide Masons throughout the world forever on this matter: *"Pure Ancient Freemasonry consists of but three degrees, that of Entered Apprentice, Fellowcraft, and Master Mason, including the Supreme Order of the Holy Royal Arch."* The Chapter of Royal Arch Masonry consists of four degrees, Mark Master, Past Master, Most Excellent Master, and Royal Arch Mason.

THE MARK MASTER DEGREE

The Mark Master Degree is believed to have originated as a ceremony of registering a craftsman's mark in those years distinguished by operative craft masons and their temple building. It was later developed into a full-fledged degree by the Masonic fraternity as we know it today,

Some scholars say it was the earliest degree and may predate all others by many years. It is highly regarded by students in all Masonry, teaching lessons that have proven of value in all walks of life. Some Grand Lodges place so high an eminence on the Mark Master Degree, that they confine it to the jurisdiction of a separate grand body, the Grand Lodge of Mark Masters.

Personal Reflections on this Degree

_____

_____

_____

_____

_____

_____

_____

_____

_____

_____

THE PAST MASTERS DEGREE

The Past Master Degree came into being because originally the degree of Royal Arch was conferred by the Symbolic (Blue) Lodge only on actual Past Masters. This degree was instituted to make it possible for all worthy Brethren to receive the Royal Arch degree. The first record of its conferral is found in 1768 in England.

Personal Reflections on this Degree

_____

_____

_____

_____

_____

_____

_____

_____

_____

_____

_____

_____

_____

THE MOST EXCELLENT MASTER DEGREE

The Most Excellent Master Degree is a product of American innovation. It was conferred in a Royal Arch Chapter as early as 1783 in Middletown, Conn. It is by far the most spectacular degree in all Freemasonry. It is the only degree that brings forcibly to our attention the completion and dedication of King Solomon's Temple.

Personal Reflections on this Degree

_____

_____

_____

_____

_____

_____

_____

_____

_____

_____

_____

_____

_____

THE ROYAL ARCH DEGREE

The Royal Arch Degree is the climax of Ancient Craft Masonry and Masonic Symbolism. It is described as "the root and marrow of Freemasonry." It is the complete story of Jewish History during some of its darkest hours. Jerusalem and the Holy temple are destroyed, The people are being held captive as slaves in Babylon. Here you will join with some slaves as they are set free to return home and engage in the noble and glorious work of rebuilding the city and the Temple of God. It is during this rebuilding that they make a discovery that brings to light the greatest treasure of a Mason --the long lost Master's Word.

Many historians have traced the earliest origins of the Royal Arch Degree to Ireland, late in the 17th century and in England in 1738, In 1752, ambulatory or military warrants for Lodges were introduced. This was instrumental in placing the Royal Arch Degree on a par with the Master Mason Degree.

Military lodges were greatly responsible for planting Freemasonry in the Colonies and also gave birth to the use of the Marl and Royal Arch degrees in the "New World." Lodge records show that the Royal Arch Degree was conferred at Fredericksburg No. 4 on December 12, 1753. George Washington was raised in this lodge a few months prior to this date.

The value of Royal Arch Masonry will be appreciated by all who are exalted to that most sublime degree, particularly by those who are seeking to complete their Masonic education. It reveals the full light of Ancient Craft Masonry, presents it as a complete system in accordance with the original plan and justly entitles you to claim the noble name of Master Mason.

Personal Reflections on this Degree

_____

_____

2 CRYPTIC MASONRY

What is a Cryptic Mason, you may ask? A Cryptic Mason is a Companion, who has been exalted to the sublime degree of the Holy Royal Arch, and to make his knowledge of the Royal Art more complete, he is greeted a Royal Master. He learns something of the Aplha, something of the Omega, and the beginning and the end.

Being faithful to his trust and diligent in the discharge of his duties to God, his country, his neighbor, and himself, he passes the summit of Ancient Craft Masonry by being entrusted with the Cardinal Virtues of a Select Master - Secrecy and silence. As an Ish-Sodi, he dangerously learns through curious zeal that Justice swiftly calls, but Mercy boldly answers. Leaving him with the realization "that embodied within the crypt lies the Soul of Freemasonry."

It is a peculiarity of the York Rite, whether intended or not by its authors, that the movement of the degrees is often historically reversed; so that as we apparently go forward in regular progression, the knowledge and light gained reflect backward upon the path we have traveled before, and degrees that seemed complete when we took them are found to require the explanation of the subsequent degrees before they can be fully understood. This is especially true of the Cryptic degrees, two of which historically precede the Royal Arch Mason degree, but which hold in reserve their valuable teachings until the candidate is ready to receive them with the most impressive effect.

The term Cryptic Masonry stems from the fact that a central feature of the Royal and Select degrees is an underground chamber or vault.

THE ROYAL MASTER DEGREE

This is the first degree of the Cryptic Rite as conferred in the United States of America. Candidates who receive the degree are impressed with its dignified ritual and relevant teachings. It contains one section which is generally regarded as an outstanding display of symbolism and content of philosophy.

The ritualistic presentations in the degree explain the articles contained in the Holy of Holies of King Solomon's Temple, including the Ark of the Covenant. A knowledge of which is essential to those who would fully understand the preceding degrees. The principal characters in the degree are Solomon and his royal assistant.

This degree symbolizes a Fellow Craft in search of further light. Hiram Abiff is still alive and imparts to the candidate the sublime teachings of useful labor on Earth and a worthy end of life. The tragedy of his untimely death is again brought forward, with the great loss suffered by the Craft.

The efforts of the candidate are eventually rewarded, and he is admitted into a secret fellowship that has been entrusted with the secrets not yet available to the majority of the Craft. This is one of the most beautiful degrees in all Masonry, with lessons so impressive that they are never forgotten.

Personal Reflections on this Degree

_____

_____

THE SELECT MASTER DEGREE

The degree of Select Master has not always been associated with hat of Royal Master. Jeremy Cross, a traveling Masonic lecturer, author, and educator of the early 1800's, is given credit by most writers for having combined the two degrees into one rite. There is strong evidence to support the theory that the degree came from a similar degree in the Scottish Rite called Intimate Secretary or Grand Tyler of King Solomon. Regardless of its origin the legend of this degree is old.

The scene of this degree is laid in the underground vault of King Solomon's Temple. The events which characterize the degree are stirring enough to make it one of intense interest. The ritualistic presentations contain the story to "complete the Circle of Perfection" in Ancient Craft Masonry.

When the Temple of Solomon was completed, a number of the secrets of the Craft had been lost. The craftsmen were advised that future generations may rediscover them if they properly applied themselves with fervency and zeal. The Select Master degree reveals how these secrets had been preserved for subsequent rediscovery.

The degree dramatizes an incident which occurred during the building of the Temple. It is closely connected with the Royal Arch Mason degree, and in fact affords the explanation needed for its perfect understanding. Our three ancient Grand Masters appear in charge of a very important work connected with the Temple. The candidate, who represents one of King Solomon's most particular friends, is promoted to the work, in which only a limited number are employed. The information imparted to the candidate makes clear to him the preceding degrees.

Personal Reflections on this Degree

_____

_____

THE SUPER EXCELLENT MASTER DEGREE

As we have stated, the degree of Super Excellent Master is not a degree of the Crypt. But, it relates events that lead to the recovery of the lost Word. This degree beautifully tells of a period in history in which all Freemasons are interested, that period following the destruction of the first Temple. The essence of the degree is foretold in the presentation by the Principal Sojourner in the Royal Arch Degree when he makes reference "Zedekiah was one and twenty years old when he began to reign and he reigned for eleven years in Jerusalem, and he did which was evil in the sight of the Lord his God," etc.

The degree of Super Excellent Master is one of the best devised, most impressive, and beautiful degrees. It is most enlightening and relevant to one's daily life. In a display of exciting events, Biblical characters come to life exemplifying the historical drama of the Holy Bible. Here Nebuchadnezzar rules again; Zedekiah proves the results of his wicked life; Ezekiel and Jeremiah prophesy the promises of Almighty God.

This degree has no connection either in history or symbolism with the Royal and Select Master degrees. It refers to circumstances that occurred during the siege of Jerusalem by Nebuzaradan, commander of the army of Babylon, and the ceremonies are intended to represent the final destruction of King Solomon's Temple and the carrying away of the captive Jews to Babylon. King Zedekiah of Judah listens to his false counselors and despises the warnings of the Prophet Jeremiah to heed his fealty to Babylon. Jerusalem is captured and its traitorous King is taken before King Nebuchadnezzar, who visits horrendous punishment upon him and his sons before utterly reducing the city and its Temple to rubble.

The Super Excellent Master degree is one of the most dramatic and impressive in all of Free masonry and is especially significant in that it is the only degree based directly upon the destruction of the Temple. In full form, it requires a large, well-rehearsed cast, and every Cryptic Mason should avail himself of an opportunity to witness the degree in full form, even if he has already received it in abbreviated form.

Personal Reflections on this Degree_____

_____

_____

_____

_____

_____

_____

_____

_____

_____

_____

_____

_____

_____

_____

3 TEMPLARY

Integrity, Obedience, Courage. The Knights Templar is a Christian-oriented fraternal organization that was founded in the 12th century. Originally, the Knights Templar were laymen who protected and defended Christians traveling to Jerusalem. These men took vows of poverty, chastity and obedience, and were renowned for their fierceness and courage in battle. Today, the Knights Templar display their courage and goodwill in other ways. They organize fund-raising activities such as breakfasts, dinners, benefits, and food drives. They support Masonic-related youth groups and they raise millions of dollars for medical research and educational assistance. Currently, Templar membership consists of people from all walks of life, all of whom profess a belief in the Christian Religion. All Knights Templar are members of the world's oldest fraternal organization known as "Free And Accepted Masons" or more commonly known as "Masons". However, not all Masons are Knights Templar. Templary is but a part of Masonry, known as the "York Rite of Freemasonry."

Qualifications and the Pilgrim's Path

Our Commandery of Knights Templar works under a Charter granted by authority of the Grand Commandery of Tennessee, York Rite Masons, for the express purpose of conferring the Orders of Christian Knighthood upon worthy and well qualified pilgrims.

Worthy and well qualified means to the Commandery that the pilgrim has successfully completed the tasks set forth in the preceding degrees of Masonry. These tasks are called the "York Rite Degrees of Masonry." There are many organizations in Masonry. However, only those who choose the Pilgrim's path will gain admission into Christian Orders of Knighthood. While the pilgrim must acknowledge their willingness to defend the Christian religion before he gains admission into our Knights Templar Asylum, the preceding Degrees of Masonry require no such election of preference. Men of all faiths that believe in the existence of a Supreme Being are welcome to travel the path through the Council. Those who do not qualify for admission into the Commandery still have plenty of opportunities in Masonry to become a Knight or even a Noble. But the distinction of a Christian Knight comes only through the Pilgrim's Path. Sounds exciting? We think so, and we can show you the way...if you ask.

Explanation of the Degrees

THE ILLUSTRIOUS ORDER OF THE RED CROSS (KNIGHT OF THE RED CROSS)

An Order emphasizing the lesson of truth. Elements of this Order were practiced in Ancient Lodges before the final form of the Master Mason Degree came into use. It is still practiced in the full ceremonial form by the Knights Masons of Ireland, the Knights Masons of the United States, and as the Red Cross of Babylon in the English Order of the Allied Masonic Degrees.

Set in the period of the Royal Arch Mason degree, a grand council is convened at Jerusalem to deliberate upon the unhappy condition of the country and to devise means to secure the favor of King Darius and his consent to proceeding with the rebuilding of the city and temple. Zerubabel, represented by the candidate, offers to travel to the Persian court and remind the King of his former promise to aid the Jews in the work. He participates in a royal debate and when his turn comes, he proclaims THE ALMIGHTY FORCE OF TRUTH. King Darius is so impressed that he grants Zerubabel his wish. Zerubabel reminds him of his vow. The King makes a decree accordingly, and to perpetuate it he creates the Order of the Red Cross, founded upon TRUTH, and confers it upon Zerubabel.

Here we bid farewell to all the degrees having to do with the building of King Solomon's Temple, its destruction, and the rebuilding of the city and temple, and we go forward to the period of the Crusades when the Orders of Knighthood were formed to recover the Holy Sepulcher and to protect the pilgrims who went to visit its sacred shrines. It is also at this point that the York Rite takes on a distinctly Christian character in which the candidate is recruited as a knightly soldier to wage war against the enemies of Christ.

Personal Reflections on this Order

_____

_____

_____

_____

_____

_____

_____

_____

_____

_____

THE ORDER OF MALTA
(KNIGHT OF MALTA)

An Order emphasizing the lesson of faith. This Order requires the Mason to profess and practice the Christian faith. The Order is centered on allegorical elements of the Knights of Malta, inheritors of the medieval Knights Hospitaller.

Order of St. Paul and the Mediterranean Pass
(Knight of St. Paul)

The pass degree of the Mediterranean Pass, or Knight of St. Paul prepares the candidate for the Order by introducing the lesson and example of the unfearing and faithful martyr of Christianity. The ceremonies of the Mediterranean Pass degree refer to the shipwreck of Saint Paul upon the island of Melita or Malta, and the viper that came out of the fire and clung to his hand, as related in the Acts of the Apostles.

Ancient and Masonic Order of St. John of Jerusalem, Palestine, Rhodes, and Malta (Knight of Malta)

The members represent soldiers of the Cross, and the Order is dedicated to Saint John the Baptist. The candidate humbly solicits to be admitted to the privilege of the Mediterranean Pass to enable him to safely undertake a pilgrimage to the Holy Sepulcher, and also to be enrolled as a Knight of Malta. The Order of Malta describes the history of the original order of Hospitallers who were famed for the construction & maintenance of hospitals for the poor.

Personal Reflections on this Order

_____

_____

_____

_____

_____

_____

_____

_____

_____

_____

THE ORDER OF THE TEMPLE (KNIGHT TEMPLAR)

An Order emphasizing the lessons of self-sacrifice and reverence. It is meant to rekindle the spirit of the medieval Knights Templar devotion and self-sacrifice to Christianity. The history of the Masonic Order is long and convoluted, with the Order's ritual differing between that conferred in England and in the United States. That practiced in the United States has a slight militant zeal to the lesson of Christianity, whereas the English ritual is more allegorical. However, the American ritual is most impressive, and more emphasis is placed on the solemnity and reverence associated with the Crucifixion, Resurrection, and Ascension of Christ. The presiding body is a Commandery, and the presiding officer is a Commander (titled Eminent).

In one of the grandest and most impressive ceremonies in all of Masonry, the true capstone of the YORK RITE, the candidate represents a knight of the period that succeeded the Crusades, who has made a vow to visit the Holy Sepulcher, and who seeks admission into the ranks of the Templars, the better to fulfill that vow. As a trial of his worthiness there is enjoined upon him seven years of preparation, beginning with an unarmed pilgrimage in the direction of the Holy Shrine. After having served six years of this preparation, he is commanded to devote the remaining year of preparation to penance, as a trial of faith and humility. Beautiful lessons of the death and ascension of our Savior are inculcated, and the candidate is at last received into full fellowship in a most solemn manner.

The ancient Order of the Temple was suppressed and its members dispersed, and the warlike spirit of the Order has passed away. But there remains a spirit of refined and moral Chivalry which prompts the members to be ever ready to defend the weak, the innocent, the hapless and the oppressed, and at last to be greeted as Brethren and received into the "widely extended arms of the blessed Emanuel".

Personal Reflections on this Order

_____

_____

_____

_____

_____

_____

_____

_____

_____

_____

_____

4 INVITATIONAL BODIES

Information extracted from the York Rite website, yorkrite.org

THE CHAIR DEGREES

The "Chair Degrees" of York Rite Masonry, so called as the candidate must be the installed or a past presiding officer of the respective York Rite body. They may also differ somewhat in name or character from one jurisdiction to another.

Order of High Priesthood

A chair degree conferred upon installed or past High Priests. Sometimes referred to as the Anointed Order of High Priesthood. In antiquity, this degree was known as the Order of Melchizadek.

Thrice Illustrious Master (Order of the Silver Trowel)

A chair degree conferred upon installed or past Illustrious Masters. It is also known as the Order of the Silver Trowel from the jewel of the degree.

Knight Crusader of the Cross

A chair degree conferred upon installed or past Eminent

Commanders.

Sovereign Order of Knights Preceptor

All present and Past Commanders of Constituent and Subordinate Commanderies of the Grand Encampment of Knights Templar of the United States of America in a jurisdiction where there is not any Chapter of the Order may petition for membership in the Order of Knights Preceptor.

The Grand Chapter of the Order of Knights Preceptor meets annually at the time and place of the Annual Meeting of the Grand Council of Allied Masonic Degrees of the United States of America.

Past Commanders Association

In some jurisdictions, an association for all present and Past Commanders of Constituent and Subordinate Commanderies of the Grand Encampment of Knights Templar of the United States of America.

APPENDANT AND ALLIED BODIES

The following bodies are appendant to the York Rite bodies due to the requirement that their members must also be members of the York Rite or one of its bodies; or are allied to the York Rite by the requirement that their members must be Masons.

First are the invitational bodies, in which the candidate must be a member of the York Rite or one of its bodies, be invited by a member of the invitational body, and pass a ballot for membership.

Second are the allied Masonic bodies, which require the candidate to be a Mason and may have additional requirements, such as being invitational or requiring other Masonic or fraternal affiliations or memberships.

Many of the following organizations are exclusive in nature and their memberships represent the more dedicated and select of the

Masonic fraternity's membership. This selectivity is usually exhibited in the limitations of the body's membership size and/or its selection processes and requirements.

UNRESTRICTED INVITATIONAL APPENDANT BODIES

These bodies are open to members of the York Rite by invitation only, but there is no restriction on the number of members allowed per body.

The York Rite Sovereign College of North America

An invitational body dedicated to the assistance and promotion of York Rite Bodies and degree work. The presiding body is a College, and the presiding officer is a Governor (titled Preeminent). The body works one main degree, that of Order of Knight of York, and one honorary degree, that of Order of the Purple Cross of York.

The Order of Knight Masons of the U.S.A.

An invitational body originally sponsored by the Knight Masons of Ireland. It is also known as the "Green Degrees." In England, the parts of the degrees are worked as part of the Order of Allied Masonic Degrees under the title of the Red Cross of Babylon. Membership once required affiliation with the Knights Templar in Ireland, but only with the Royal Arch in the U.S.A. The presiding body is a Council, and the presiding officer is a Chief (titled Excellent).

Degrees worked are:

- Knight of Sword
- Knight of the East
- Knight of the East and West
- Installed Chief (Chair Degree)

Knights of the York Cross of Honour (KYCH)

An invitational body composed entirely of York Rite Masonic

leaders. Members must be a Past Master of a Symbolic Lodge, a Past High Priest of a Royal Arch Chapter, a Past Master of a Royal and Select Masters Council, and a Past Commander of a Knight Templar Commandery; and nominated by a KYCH. A past Grand presiding officer receives the title of Knight of the York Grand Cross of Honour (KYGCH) if he serves in such a capacity after becoming a KYCH. Membership is unlimited in the presiding body. The presiding body is a Priory, and the presiding officer is a Prior (titled Eminent).

The Commemorative Order of St. Thomas of Acon

An invitational body composed of York Rite Masons selected for their contributions and dedication to the Masonic bodies and orders. Membership requires affiliation with the Knights Templar. The modern Order commemoratives an early body of English Knights Templar founded during the 3rd Crusade. Membership is unlimited in the presiding body. The presiding body is a Chapel, and the presiding officer is a Master (titled Worthy).

RESTRICTIVE INVITATIONAL APPENDANT BODIES

These bodies are open to members of the York Rite by invitation only, with strict limitations on the number of members allowed per body.

The Allied Masonic Degrees (AMD)

An invitational body dedicated to the preservation and exemplification of Masonic side degrees of antiquity.

EDITOR's NOTE: In some jurisdictions the AMD Councils are limited to presenting research papers.

Membership requires affiliation with the Royal Arch and is limited to 27 members per presiding body. The presiding body is a Council, and the presiding officer is a Sovereign Master (titled Venerable). European AMD Councils open and transact business on the Order of St. Lawrence the Martyr.

In addition to the AMD Council, there are two subordinate bodies attached to the Council, which operate as separate bodies outside the United States.

Degrees worked are:

- Order of St. Lawrence the Martyr
- Knight of Constantinople
- Grand Tylers of Solomon
- Excellent Master
- Masters of Tyre
- Architect
- Grand Architect
- Superintendent
- Ye Antient Order of the Corks
- Red Branch of Eri and Appendant Orders (Honorary)
- Royal Ark Mariner (separate Lodge outside the USA)
- Order of the Secret Monitor (separate Conclave outside the USA)
- Installed Sovereign Master (AMD Chair Degree)
- Installed Master (OStLM Chair Degree)
- Installed Commander Noah (RAM Chair Degree)
- Installed Supreme Ruler (OSM Chair Degree)

The Red Cross of Constantine & Appendant Orders (RCC)

An invitational body composed of highly dedicated and long serving York Rite Masons. Membership requires affiliation with the Royal Arch, and belief in the Trinitarian Christian faith. Membership is limited to 45 members per presiding body. The presiding body is a Conclave, and the presiding officer is a Sovereign (titled Puissant).

Degrees worked are:

- Knight of the Red Cross of Constantine
- Knight of the Holy Sepulchre
- Knight of St. John the Evangelist

- Installed Viceroy (Chair Degree)
- Installed Sovereign (Chair Degree)

The Order of Holy Royal Arch Knight Templar Priests (HRAKTP)

An invitational body composed of highly dedicated and long serving York Rite Masons. Membership requires affiliation with the Knights Templar, and members must be Past Eminent Commanders of a Knight Templar Commandery. Originally, this body conferred 33 degrees, but now only one is conferred. Membership is limited to 27 members per presiding body. The presiding body is a Tabernacle, and the presiding officer is a Preceptor (titled Eminent).

ADDITIONAL MASONIC ORGANIZATIONS

The following lists some of the additional Masonic organizations found in the Masonic family. Included are the bodies of Adoptive Masonry and Masonic sponsored youth organizations. It does not list the other organizations allied to Masonry such as the AAONMS, Shriners, Daughters of the Nile, Tall Cedars of Lebanon, or Grotto.

Research and Fellowship Bodies

These bodies are open in membership to any Mason. They exist as Masonic research and social fellowship groups.

The Philalethes Society

A Masonic research society that is open to Masons and is dedicated to Masonic research. This body includes many noted Masonic authors and researchers. The presiding body is the Society, and the presiding officer is a President.

The Grand College of Rites of the United States of America

A Masonic research society that is open to Master Masons and is dedicated to the study, history, and preservation of extinct

Masonic Rites, rituals, and ceremonies. The membership of this body is predominately composed of York Rite Masons. The body gathers annually for the transaction of business and the presentation of papers. The presiding body is the Grand College, and the presiding officer is a Grand Chancellor (titled Most Illustrious).

The Society of Blue Friars

An invitational Masonic literary body whose membership is composed solely of published Masonic authors, and limited to 20 members. It is unique in its honorary status, there being no fees or membership dues assessed, and its members retain membership ad vita. The presiding body is the Society and the presiding officer is a Grand Abbot (titled Most Illustrious).

The Masonic Order of the Bath

Qualifications for membership:

1) You must be a Master Mason in good standing in Lodges recognized as "regular."
2) There IS NO #2.

The presiding officer is titled "Most Honorable Commander-General". Generally meets in Washington DC as part of Masonic Week.

The High Twelve International

A Masonic luncheon club, open to Masons currently expanded to three Countries. The name of the organization derives from a Masonic term meaning noon. Its stated purpose is to inculcate the ideals taught in Masonry by uniting in the happy bonds of a fraternal hour, those ideals being the strengthening of Masonic ties, participation in community activities, and the furtherance of the public school system. There are no degrees, ritual, or ceremonies. It fulfills the role of the "Table Lodges" found in some jurisdictions, but without the formality or ritual associated with those organizations. The presiding body is a Club, and the presiding officer is a President.

Historical Invitational Bodies

These bodies preserve the unique Masonic history and heritage associated with colonial and early American Masonry.

The National Sojourners, Inc.

An invitational body composed of Masons who are or were commissioned, warrant, or senior non-commissioned officers in the Armed Forces of the United States of America, and dedicated to the preservation and perpetuation of the Masonic fraternal heritage and its history in the Armed Forces of the United States of America. Provisions exist for the admission of honorary members who do not meet the prerequisite qualifications.

This body inculcates the principles of the former English and American "military" Lodges, which operated under lawful Craft warrants from the 1700's through the early 1900's. The Grand Lodge of the Philippines was organized as a result of the efforts and work of this body. A side body of the Sojourners is the Heroes of '76. The presiding body is a Chapter, and the presiding officer is a President.

INVITATIONAL BODIES OF THE ANCIENT AND ACCEPTED SCOTTISH RITE

The Royal Order of Scotland occupies a unique place in American Masonry, as it is controlled by the Grand Lodge of Scotland, and was "usurped" in a sense when Albert Pike was appointed the Provincial Grand Master and allied it with the A.A.S.R. However, the statues in the U.S.A. still conform to those of the mother Grand Lodge and the body is open to 32° Scottish Rite Masons by invitation and Knights Templar by special waiver.

The Royal Order of Scotland (ROS)

An invitational body composed of highly dedicated and long serving Scottish Rite Masons. While allied with and considered a Scottish Rite Degree in the United States, this Order was once under the jurisdiction of the York Rite, being controlled by the Grand Lodge of Scotland, and as a result of this former disposition, it is also open to Knights Templar by waiver of the Provincial Grand Master. Membership requires affiliation with the Scottish Rite (32°) and a Trinitarian Christian, or a Knight Templar; and the recommendation of a member.

This is the only Masonic body that is considered to be an authentic Royal Order. The Degree of Knight of the Rosy Cross is believed to contain remnants of the original investiture ceremony of the Most Ancient and Most Noble Order of the Thistle, the Royal Scottish Dynastic Order. The Masonic body is under the jurisdiction of the Grand Lodge of Scotland. In the United States of America, the body operates as a Provincial Grand Lodge, and the presiding officer is a Provincial Grand Master. It is unlimited in membership.

The two degrees worked are:

- Degree of Heredom of Kilwinning
- Degree of Knight of the Rosy Cross

INVITATIONAL BODIES OF ULTRA-CRAFT MASONRY

Ultra-craft Masonic bodies are those that simply lie outside of those of the Rites, or in simpler terms, requiring only Masonic affiliation with a recognized Masonic Blue Lodge. Technically, every appendant body is part of ultra-craft masonry, though here the term is used in connection with bodies not controlled by either of the two Rites of the United States.

The Societas Rosicruciana in Civitatibus Foederatis (SRICF)

An invitational body composed of highly dedicated and long serving Masons, and dedicated to the esoteric and philosophical study and examination of Masonry. Membership requires affiliation with a Symbolic Lodge, and a profession of the Christian faith. While membership in the York Rite Bodies is not necessarily required, most of the members of the SRICF often hold membership in the York Rite and many of its appendant bodies. This body is in fraternal amity with the Masonic Societas Rosicruciana in Anglia (England), the Masonic Societas Rosicruciana in Scotia (Scotland), the Masonic Societas Rosicruciana in Gallia (France), and the Masonic Societas Rosicruciana in Portugallia (Portugal). Advancement to the higher degrees within the body is determined upon merit and service. Membership is limited to 72 members per presiding body. The presiding body is a College, and the presiding officer is a Chief Adept (titled Worthy).

Degrees worked are:

- I   Zelator
- II   Theoricus
- III   Practicus
- IV   Philosophus
- V   Adeptus Minor
- VI   Adeptus Major
- VII   Adeptus Exemptus
- VIII   Magister Templi
- IX   Magus

AFFILIATED ADOPTIVE MASONIC BODIES

These are Masonic organizations whose memberships include both men and women in their bodies. The York Rite is an active participant and supporter in Adoptive Masonic bodies.

The Order of the Amaranth

An Adoptive Masonic organization. The organization was founded in 1873. Membership is limited to Masons, their spouses, and female relatives. It was originally intended to be an additional degree of the Order of the Eastern Star, but was rejected by that organization. It was then set up as a separate organization. Until 1921, members had to be affiliated with the Order of the Eastern

Star. The presiding body is a Court, and the presiding female and male officers are a Royal Matron and Royal Patron.

The Order of the Eastern Star (OES)

An Adoptive Masonic organization. The organization was founded in 1857. Membership is limited to Masons, their spouses, and female relatives. Meetings require the presence of a Mason in order to open and transact business. The presiding body is a Chapter, and the presiding female and male officers are a Worthy Matron and Worthy Patron.

Degrees worked are:

- Obedience (Adah)
- Devotion (Ruth)
- Fidelity (Esther)
- Faith (Martha)
- Charity (Electa)

The Order of the White Shrine of Jerusalem

An Adoptive Masonic organization. The organization was founded in 1894. Membership is limited to Masons, their spouses, and female relatives. Members must profess the Christian faith. Meetings require the presence of a Mason in order to open and transact business. The presiding body is a Shrine, and the presiding female and male officers are a High Priestess and Watchman of Shepherds.

Social Order of the Beauceant (S.O.O.B.)

As the wives, widows, mothers, daughters and sisters of Knights Templars, they are the only ladies' fraternal order whose eligibility is determined by the husband's membership in the Commandery.

A new Assembly may be constituted wherever there is an active Commandery of Knights Templar of sufficient size to warrant it, and there are several eligible ladies.

MASONIC YOUTH ORGANIZATIONS

These organizations are youth organizations sponsored and supported by the Masonic bodies. The York Rite is extremely active in its involvement with these groups.

The Order of DeMolay (IODM)

A Masonic youth organization for young men aged 12 to 21 years. Membership does not require family Masonic affiliation, nor does it confer any Masonic membership. The organization is dedicated to providing guidance and development of civic leadership and social values in young men. A side body of the DeMolay is the Order of Knighthood. The presiding body is a Chapter, and the presiding officer is a Master Councilor.

Degrees worked include:

- Initiatory Degree
- DeMolay Degree
- Degree of Chevalier (Honorary Degree)

The Order of Job's Daughters (IOJD)

A Masonic youth organization for young women aged 10 to 20 years. Membership is limited to girls with a male Masonic relative. The organization is dedicated to the development of civic leadership and social values in young women. The presiding body is a Bethel, and the presiding officer is an Honored Queen.

Iinitiation ceremony that is separated into three "epochs":

- First Epoch
- Second Epoch
- Third Epoch

The Order of the Rainbow for Girls (IORG)

A Masonic youth organization for young women aged 12 to 20

years. Membership does not require Masonic affiliation, nor does it confer Masonic membership. The organization is dedicated to the development of civic leadership and social values in young women. The presiding body is an Assembly, and the presiding officer is a Worthy Advisor. There is one main degree, that of the Initiation Degree, and one honorary degree, that of the Grand Cross of Colors Degree.

The Invitational Bodies of York Rite Masonry

Fig. 4-1

5 MASONIC FORMS OF ADDRESS

With such diverseness within the content of the various bodies of the York and Scottish Rite bodies, there comes a confusion as to who is who. This chapter lists the various titles of office within the primary bodies and provides their basic operating hierarchies.

GRAND LODGE OF FREEMASONS

GRAND OFFICER TITLES

Most Worshipful Grand Master
Right Worshipful Deputy Grand Master
Right Worshipful Senior Grand Warden
Right Worshipful Junior Grand Warden
Most Worshipful Past Grand Master
Right Worshipful Grand Treasurer
Right Worshipful Grand Secretary
Right Worshipful Grand Chaplain
Worshipful Senior Grand Deacon
Worshipful Junior Grand Deacon
Worshipful Grand Marshal
Worshipful Grand Sword Bearer
Worshipful Grand Steward
Worshipful Grand Pursuivant
Worshipful Grand Tyler

Worshipful Grand Historian
Worshipful Grand Organist
Worshipful Grand Photographer
Worshipful Grand Lecturer
Past Worshipful Master

LOCAL BODY TITLES

Worshipful Master
Senior Warden
Junior Warden
Treasurer
Past Worshipful Master
Secretary
Chaplain
Senior Deacon
Junior Deacon
Tyler
Marshal
Trustees

GRAND CHAPTER, ROYAL ARCH MASONS

GRAND OFFICER TITLES

Most Excellent Grand High Priest
Right Excellent Grand King
Right Excellent Grand Scribe
Most Excellent Past Grand High Priest
Right Excellent Grand Treasurer
Right Excellent Grand Secretary
Right Excellent Grand Chaplain
Excellent Grand Captain of the Host
Excellent Grand Principal Sojourner
Excellent Grand Royal Arch Captain
Excellent Grand Master of the 1st veil
Excellent Grand Master of the 2nd Veil
Excellent Grand Master of the 3rd veil
Grand Sentinel

District Deputy Grand High Priests

LOCAL BODY TITLES

High Priest
King
Scribe
Past High Priest
Treasurer
Secretary
Chaplain
Captain of the Host
Principal Sojourner
Royal Arch Captain
Master of the 1st veil
Master of the 2nd Veil
Master of the 3rd veil
Sentinel
Key Man

GRAND COUNCIL, CRYPTIC MASONS (ROYAL & SELECT MASTERS)

GRAND OFFICER TITLES

Most Illustrious Grand Master
Right Illustrious Deputy Grand Master
Right Illustrious Grand Principal Conductor of the Work
Most Illustrious Past Grand Master
Right Illustrious Grand Treasurer
Right Illustrious Grand Recorder
Illustrious Grand Captain of the Guard
Illustrious Grand Conductor of the Council
Illustrious Grand Steward
Illustrious Grand Chaplain
Illustrious Grand Marshal
Illustrious Grand Sentinel
Grand Masters Personal Representatives
Grand Instructors

LOCAL BODY TITLES

Illustrious Master
Deputy Master
Principal Conductor of the Work
Past Illustrious Master
Treasurer
Recorder
Captain of the Guard
Conductor of the Council
Steward
Chaplain
Marshal
Sentinel
Key Man

GRAND COMMANDERY, KNIGHTS TEMPLAR

GRAND OFFICER TITLES

Right Eminent Grand Commander
Very Eminent Deputy Grand Commander
Eminent Grand Generalissimo
Eminent Grand Captain General
Right Eminent Past Grand Commander
Eminent Grand Senior Warden
Eminent Grand Junior Warden
Eminent Grand Prelate
Eminent Grand Treasurer
Eminent Grand Recorder
Eminent Grand Standard Bearer
Eminent Grand Sword Bearer
Eminent Grand Warder
Eminent Grand Sentinel
Past Grand Department Commander

LOCAL BODY TITLES

Eminent Commander

Generalissimo
Captain General
Past Commander
Senior Warden
Junior Warden
Prelate
Treasurer
Recorder
Standard Bearer
Sword Bearer
Warder
Sentinel
Guard (x3)

GRAND ENCAMPMENT, KNIGHTS TEMPLAR

Most Eminent Grand Master
Right Eminent Deputy Grand Master
Right Eminent Grand Generalissimo
Right Eminent Grand Captain General
Most Eminent Past Grand Master
Right Eminent Grand Senior Warden
Right Eminent Grand Junior Warden
Right Eminent Grand Prelate
Right Eminent Grand Treasurer
Right Eminent Grand Recorder
Right Eminent Grand Standard Bearer
Right Eminent Grand Sword Bearer
Right Eminent Grand Warder
Right Eminent Grand Sentinel
Right Eminent Grand Marshal
Right Eminent Deprtment Commander
Right Eminent Past Grand Officer
Right Eminent Past Department Commander

YORK RITE COLLEGE (YRC)

GRAND OFFICER TITLES

Past Grand Governor
Grand Governor
Deputy Grand Governor
Deputy Grand Governor

LOCAL BODY TITLES

Past Eminent Governor
Preeminent Governor
Eminent Deputy Governor
Eminent Chancellor
Eminent Treasurer
Eminent Secretary
Noble Primate
Noble Preceptor
Noble Seneschal
Noble Marshal
Noble Sentinel

GRAND COUNCIL, KNIGHTS MASON USA

KCZ – Knight Commander of Zerubbabel (Honor)

GRAND OFFICER TITLES

Most Excellent Past Grand Chief
Most Excellent Grand Chief
Right Excellent Deputy Grand Chief
Right Excellent Grand Senior Warden
Right Excellent Junior Warden
Right Excellent Grand Scribe
Right Excellent Grand Treasurer
Very Excellent Grand Senior Warden
Very Excellent Junior Warden
Very Excellent Grand Director of Ceremonies

Very Excellent Grand Priest
Very Excellent Grand Steward
Very Excellent Grand Sentinel
Right Excellent Grand Musician
Excellent Chief of Great Chief's

LOCAL BODY TITLES

Excellent Chief
Senior Knight
Junior Knight
Secretary
Treasurer
Senior Warden
Junior Warden
Director of Ceremonies
Priest
First Guard
Sentinel

ACRONYMS for YORK RITE HONORS

GRAND OFFICER TITLES

KCC – Knight Crusader of the Cross
KCT – Knight Commander of the Temple
KGC – Knight Grand Cross (Grand Encampment)
KTCH – Knight Templar Cross of Honor
KYCH – Knight York Cross of Honor
KYGCH – Knight York Grand Cross of Honor

LOCAL BODY TITLES

RCC – Red Cross of Constantine
RIC – Rosicrucian (Societas Rosicruciana)
ROS – Royal Order of Scotland
RTB – Robert The Bruce
OPC – Order of the Purple Cross
4BL – Order of the Four Black Lamas (For fun)

ALLIED MASONIC DEGREES

GRAND OFFICER TITLES

Past Sovereign Grand Master
Sovereign Grand Master
Knight Grand Cross
Knight Branch of Eri
Sovereign Master
Supreme Ruler of the Secret Monitor
Worshipful Master-St. Lawrence the Martyr
Commander Noah-Royal Ark Mariner

LOCAL BODY TITLES

Sovereign Master
Senior Warden
Junior Warden
Senior Deacon
Junior Deacon
Chaplain
Secretary
Treasurer
Tyler

CONVENT GENERAL - KYCH

GRAND OFFICER TITLES

Grand Master General
Deputy Grand Master-General
Grand Warder of the Temple
Past Grand Master General
Grand Treasurer-General
Grand Registrar-General
Grand Seneschal
Grand Marshal
Grand Sentinel
Grand Prelate

LOCAL BODY TITLES (PRIORY)

Eminent Prior
Deputy Prior
Warder
Past Prior
Registrar-Treasurer
Prelate
Orator
Herald

GRAND COUNCIL
ORDER of HIGH PRIESTHOOD

Most Excellent Grand President
Most Excellent Grand Vice President
Most Excellent Grand Chaplain
Most Excellent Grand Recorder-Treasurer
Most Excellent Master of Ceremonies
Most Excellent Grand Conductor
Most Excellent Grand Herald
Most Excellent Grand Steward
Most Excellent Grand Sentinel
Most Excellent Past Grand President

ORDER OF THE SILVER TROWEL

Illustrious King
Illustrious Prince of the West
Illustrious Prince of the South
Illustrious Treasurer-Scribe
Illustrious Prince of the Court
Illustrious Captain of the Guard
Illustrious Chaplain
Past Illustrious King

SHRINE

Illustrious Potentate
Chief Rabban
Assistant Rabban
Past Illustrious Potentate
High Priest and Prophet
Oriental Guide
Treasurer
Recorder

SCOTTISH RITE HONORS

KCCH – Knight Commander Court of Honor
33rd Degree
Grand Cross of the Court of Honor

ANCIENT & ACCEPTED SCOTTISH RITE

GRAND OFFICER TITLES

Sovereign Grand Commander
Sovereign Grand Inspector General (SGIG)
Deputy Inspector General

LOCAL BODY TITLES

Personal Representative of SGIG
Venerable Master - Lodge of Perfection
Assistant Representative of the Deputy
Wise Master – Chapter of Rose Croix
Preceptor – Council of Kadosh
Master of Kadosh
Executive Secretary
Treasurer
Almoner
Director Extension
Tyler

STRUCTURE & ORGANIZATION OF FREEMASONRY

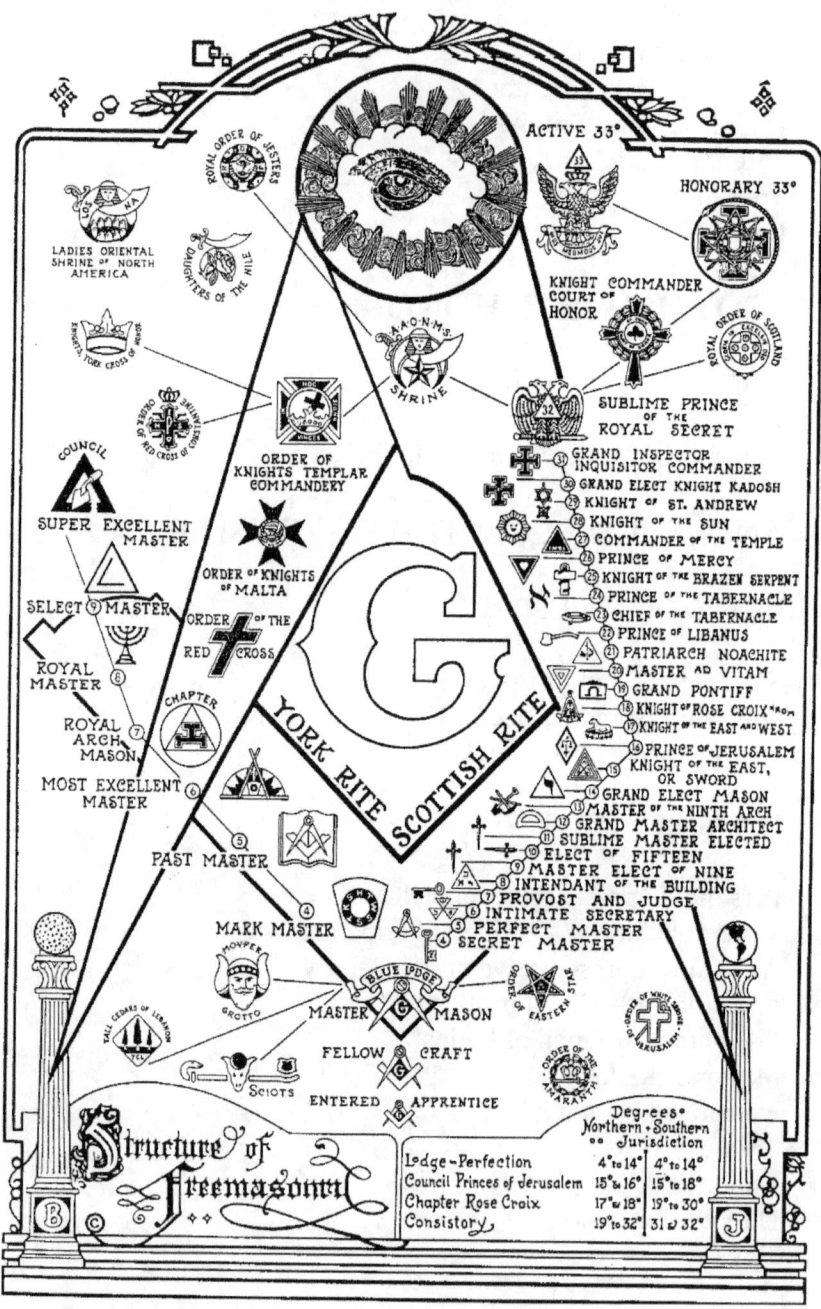

6 YORK RITE DEGREE RECORD

Presented_____ **Elected**_____

Lodge_____ **No.**_____

THE SYMBOLIC DEGREES (CRAFT/BLUE LODGE)

Entered Apprentice

Date_____ Location_____

Body_____ No. _____

Fellow Craft

Date_____ Location_____

Body_____ No. _____

Master Mason

Date_____ Location_____

Body_____ No. _____

THE CAPITULAR DEGREES (CHAPTER)

Mark Master

Date_____ Location_____

Body_____ No. _____

Past Master

Date_____ Location_____

Body_____ No. _____

Most Excellent Master

Date_____ Location_____

Body_____ No. _____

Royal Arch

Date_____ Location_____

Body_____ No. _____

THE CRYPTIC DEGREES (COUNCIL)

Royal Master Degree

Date_____ Location_____

Body_____ No. _____

Select Master Degree

Date_____ Location_____

Body_____ No. _____

Super Excellent Master

Date_____ Location_____

Body_____ No. _____

THE CHIVALRIC ORDERS (COMMANDERY)

The Illustrious Order of the Red Cross

Knight of the Red Cross

Date_____ Location_____

Body_____ No. _____

The Order of Malta

Knight of St. Paul

Date_____ Location_____

Body_____ No. _____

Knight of Malta

Date_____ Location_____

Body_____ No. _____

The Order of the Temple

Knight Templar

Date_____ Location_____

Body_____ No. _____

THE CHAIR DEGREES

Order of High Priesthood

Date_____ Location_____

Body_____ No. _____

Thrice Illustrious Master

Date_____ Location_____

Body_____ No. _____

Knight Crusader of the Cross

Date_____ Location_____

Body_____ No. _____

Sovereign Order of Knights Preceptor

Date_____ Location_____

Body_____ No. _____

Past Commanders Association

Date_____ Location_____

Body_____ No. _____

Other

Degree_____

Date_____ Location_____

Body_____ No. _____

Other

Degree_____

Date_____ Location_____

Body_____ No. _____

UNRESTRICTED INVITATIONAL APPENDANT BODIES

The York Rite Sovereign College of North America

Date_____ Location_____

Body_____ No._____

The Order of Knight Masons of the U.S.A.

Knight of Sword

Date_____ Location_____

Body_____ No._____

Knight of the East

Date_____ Location_____

Body_____ No._____

Knight of the East and West

Date_____ Location_____

Body_____ No._____

Installed Chief (Chair Degree)

Date_____ Location_____

Body_____ No._____

Knights of the York Cross of Honour (KYCH)

Date_____ Location_____

Body_____ No._____

The Commemorative Order of St. Thomas of Acon

Date_____ Location_____

Body_____ No._____

RESTRICTED INVITATIONAL APPENDANT BODIES

The Allied Masonic Degrees (AMD)

Order of St. Lawrence the Martyr

Date_____ Location_____

Body_____ No._____

Knight of Constantinople

Date_____ Location_____

Body_____ No._____

Grand Tilers of Solomon

Date_____ Location_____

Body_____ No._____

Excellent Master

Date_____ Location_____

Body_____ No._____

Masters of Tyre

Date_____ Location_____

Body_____ No._____

Architect

Date_____ Location_____

Body_____ No._____

Grand Architect

Date_____ Location_____

Body_____ No._____

Superintendent

Date_____ Location_____

Body_____ No._____

Ye Antient Order of the Corks

Date_____ Location_____

Body_____ No._____

Red Branch of Eri and Appendant Orders (Honorary Degree)

Date_____ Location_____

Body_____ No._____

Royal Ark Mariner (separate Lodge outside the USA)

Date_____ Location_____

Body_____ No._____

Order of the Secret Monitor (separate Conclave outside the USA)

Date_____ Location_____

Body_____ No._____

Installed Sovereign Master (AMD Chair Degree)

Date_____ Location_____

Body_____ No._____

Installed Master (OStLM Chair Degree)

Date_____ Location_____

Body_____ No._____

Installed Commander Noah (RAM Chair Degree)

Date_____ Location_____

Body_____ No._____

Installed Supreme Ruler (OSM Chair Degree)

Date_____ Location_____

Body_____ No._____

The Red Cross of Constantine and Appendant Orders (RCC)

Knight of the Red Cross of Constantine

Date_____ Location_____

Body_____ No._____

Knight of the Holy Sepulchre

Date_____ Location_____

Body_____ No._____

Knight of St. John the Evangelist

Date_____ Location_____

Body_____ No._____

Installed Viceroy (Chair Degree)

Date_____ Location_____

Body_____ No._____

Installed Sovereign (Chair Degree)

Date_____ Location_____

Body_____ No._____

The Order of Holy Royal Arch Knight Templar Priest (HRAKTP)

Date_____ Location_____

Body_____ No._____

The Masonic Order of the Bath

Date_____ Location_____

Body_____ No._____

INVITATIONAL BODIES OF THE ANCIENT AND ACCEPTED SCOTTISH RITE

The Royal Order of Scotland (ROS)

Degree of Heredom of Kilwinning

Date_____ Location_____

Body_____   No._____

Degree of Knight of the Rosy Cross

Date_____ Location_____

Body_____   No._____

INVITATIONAL BODIES OF ULTRA-CRAFT MASONRY

The Societas Rosicruciana in Civitatibus Foederatis (SRICF)

I Zelator

Date_____ Location_____

Body_____ No._____

II Theoricus

Date_____ Location_____

Body_____ No._____

III Practicus

Date_____ Location_____

Body_____ No._____

IV Philosophus

Date_____ Location_____

Body_____ No._____

V Adeptus Minor

Date_____ Location_____

Body_____ No._____

VI Adeptus Major

Date_____ Location_____

Body_____ No._____

VII Adeptus Exemptus

Date_____ Location_____

Body_____ No._____

VIII Magister Templi

Date_____ Location_____

Body_____ No._____

IX Magus

Date_____ Location_____

Body_____ No._____

7 OTHER DEGREES RECORD

You may use this space to record degrees that you have received that are not otherwise listed in this book.

SCOTTISH RITE LODGE OF PERFECTION DEGREES

Date_____

In _____ Lodge of Perfection

Valley_____

SCOTTISH RITE CHAPTER DEGREES

Date_____

In _____ Chapter of Rose Croix

Valley_____

SCOTTISH RITE COUNCIL DEGREES

Date_____

In _____ Council of Kadosh

Valley_____

SCOTTISH RITE CONSISTORY DEGREES

Date_____

In _____ Consistory

Valley_____

Degree_____

Date_____ Location_____

Body_____ No. _____

Degree_____

Date_____ Location_____

Body_____ No. _____

Degree_____

Date_____ Location_____

Body_____ No. _____

Degree_____

Date_____ Location_____

Body_____ No. _____

Degree_____

Date_____ Location_____

Body_____ No. _____

Degree_____

Date_____ Location_____

Body_____ No. _____

Degree_____

Date_____ Location_____

Body_____ No. _____

Degree_____

Date_____ Location_____

Body_____ No. _____

Degree_____

Date_____ Location_____

Body_____ No. _____

Degree_____

Date_____ Location_____

Body_____ No. _____

Degree_____

Date_____ Location_____

Body_____ No. _____

Degree_____

Date_____ Location_____

Body_____ No. _____

Degree_____

Date_____ Location_____

Body_____ No. _____

Degree_____

Date_____ Location_____

Body_____ No. _____

Degree_____

Date_____ Location_____

Body_____ No. _____

Degree_____

Date_____ Location_____

Body_____ No. _____

Degree_____

Date_____ Location_____

Body_____ No. _____

Degree_____

Date_____ Location_____

Body_____ No. _____

Degree_____

Date_____ Location_____

Body_____ No. _____

Degree_____

Date_____ Location_____

Body_____ No. _____

Degree_____

Date_____ Location_____

Body_____ No. _____

Degree_____

Date_____ Location_____

Body_____ No. _____

Degree_____

Date_____ Location_____

Body_____ No. _____

Degree_____

Date_____ Location_____

Body_____ No. _____

Degree_____

Date_____ Location_____

Body_____ No. _____

Degree_____

Date_____ Location_____

Body_____ No. _____

Degree_____

Date_____ Location_____

Body_____ No. _____

Degree_____

Date_____ Location_____

Body_____ No. _____

Degree_____

Date_____ Location_____

Body_____ No. _____

Degree_____

Date_____ Location_____

Body_____ No. _____

Degree_____

Date_____ Location_____

Body_____ No. _____

Degree_____

Date_____ Location_____

Body_____ No. _____

Degree_____

Date_____ Location_____

Body_____ No. _____

Degree_____

Date_____ Location_____

Body_____ No. _____

Degree_____

Date_____ Location_____

Body_____ No. _____

Degree_____

Date_____ Location_____

Body_____ No. _____

Degree_____

Date_____ Location_____

Body_____ No. _____

Degree_____

Date_____ Location_____

Body_____ No. _____

Degree_____

Date_____ Location_____

Body_____ No. _____

Degree_____

Date_____ Location_____

Body_____ No. _____

Degree_____

Date_____ Location_____

Body_____ No. _____

Degree_____

Date_____ Location_____

Body_____ No. _____

8 OFFICES HELD

You may list the offices, dates, and special appointments you have held in various Masonic bodies. If you are actively involved in several bodies, you will want to record your service and progression through the ranks. This serves as a backup record and personal tracker for you.

BODY_____

Dates   Office Held/Appointment Received

_____   _____

_____   _____

_____   _____

_____   _____

_____   _____

_____   _____

_____   _____

_____   _____

_____   _____

_____   _____

_____   _____

_____   _____

_____   _____

_____   _____

_____   _____

BODY_____

Dates   Office Held/Appointment Received

_____   _____

_____   _____

_____   _____

_____   _____

_____   _____

_____   _____

_____   _____

_____   _____

_____   _____

_____   _____

_____   _____

_____   _____

_____   _____

_____   _____

_____   _____

BODY

Dates   Office Held/Appointment Received

_____   _____

_____   _____

_____   _____

_____   _____

_____   _____

_____   _____

_____   _____

_____   _____

_____   _____

_____   _____

_____   _____

_____   _____

_____   _____

_____   _____

_____   _____

BODY_____

Dates   Office Held/Appointment Received

_____

_____

_____

_____

BODY

Dates

Office Held/Appointment Received

_____ _____

_____ _____

_____ _____

_____ _____

_____ _____

_____ _____

_____ _____

_____ _____

_____ _____

_____ _____

_____ _____

_____ _____

_____ _____

_____ _____

BODY_____

Dates   Office Held/Appointment Received

_____   _____

_____   _____

_____   _____

_____   _____

_____   _____

_____   _____

_____   _____

_____   _____

_____   _____

_____   _____

_____   _____

_____   _____

_____   _____

_____   _____

_____   _____

BODY_____

Dates   Office Held/Appointment Received

_____   _____

_____   _____

_____   _____

_____   _____

_____   _____

_____   _____

_____   _____

_____   _____

_____   _____

_____   _____

_____   _____

_____   _____

_____   _____

_____   _____

_____   _____

BODY_____

Dates   Office Held/Appointment Received

_____   _____

_____   _____

_____   _____

_____   _____

_____   _____

_____   _____

_____   _____

_____   _____

_____   _____

_____   _____

_____   _____

_____   _____

_____   _____

_____   _____

BODY_____

Dates   Office Held/Appointment Received

_____   _____

_____   _____

_____   _____

_____   _____

_____   _____

_____   _____

_____   _____

_____   _____

_____   _____

_____   _____

_____   _____

_____   _____

_____   _____

_____   _____

_____   _____

BODY_____

Dates   Office Held/Appointment Received

_____   _____

_____   _____

_____   _____

_____   _____

_____   _____

_____   _____

_____   _____

_____   _____

_____   _____

_____   _____

_____   _____

_____   _____

_____   _____

_____   _____

_____   _____

_____   _____

BODY_____

Dates   Office Held/Appointment Received

_____   _____

_____   _____

_____   _____

_____   _____

_____   _____

_____   _____

_____   _____

_____   _____

_____   _____

_____   _____

_____   _____

_____   _____

_____   _____

_____   _____

BODY_____

Dates   Office Held/Appointment Received

_____   _____

_____   _____

_____   _____

_____   _____

_____   _____

_____   _____

_____   _____

_____   _____

_____   _____

_____   _____

_____   _____

_____   _____

_____   _____

_____   _____

_____   _____

_____   _____

BODY_____

Dates   Office Held/Appointment Received

_____   _____

_____   _____

_____   _____

_____   _____

_____   _____

_____   _____

_____   _____

_____   _____

_____   _____

_____   _____

_____   _____

_____   _____

_____   _____

_____   _____

_____   _____

_____   _____

_____   _____

BODY

Dates   Office Held/Appointment Received

_____   _____

_____   _____

_____   _____

_____   _____

_____   _____

_____   _____

_____   _____

_____   _____

_____   _____

_____   _____

_____   _____

_____   _____

_____   _____

_____   _____

_____   _____

_____   _____

_____   _____

BODY

Dates	Office Held/Appointment Received
_____	_____
_____	_____
_____	_____
_____	_____
_____	_____
_____	_____
_____	_____
_____	_____
_____	_____
_____	_____
_____	_____
_____	_____
_____	_____
_____	_____

BODY_____

Dates   Office Held/Appointment Received

_____   _____

_____   _____

_____   _____

_____   _____

_____   _____

_____   _____

_____   _____

_____   _____

_____   _____

_____   _____

_____   _____

_____   _____

_____   _____

_____   _____

_____   _____

_____   _____

BODY_____

Dates   Office Held/Appointment Received

_____   _____

_____   _____

_____   _____

_____   _____

_____   _____

_____   _____

_____   _____

_____   _____

_____   _____

_____   _____

_____   _____

_____   _____

_____   _____

_____   _____

_____   _____

BODY_____

Dates   Office Held/Appointment Received

_____   _____

_____   _____

_____   _____

_____   _____

_____   _____

_____   _____

_____   _____

_____   _____

_____   _____

_____   _____

_____   _____

_____   _____

_____   _____

_____   _____

_____   _____

_____   _____

BODY_____

Dates   Office Held/Appointment Received

_____   _____

_____   _____

_____   _____

_____   _____

_____   _____

_____   _____

_____   _____

_____   _____

_____   _____

_____   _____

_____   _____

_____   _____

_____   _____

_____   _____

_____   _____

_____   _____

9 DEGREE WORK/ATTENDANCE

In this section you may list the various degree work you have attended and/or worked in for the various Masonic bodies you are involved with.

DEGREE_____

Date	Location	Worked?
_____	_____	❏ Y ❏ N
_____	_____	❏ Y ❏ N
_____	_____	❏ Y ❏ N
_____	_____	❏ Y ❏ N
_____	_____	❏ Y ❏ N
_____	_____	❏ Y ❏ N
_____	_____	❏ Y ❏ N
_____	_____	❏ Y ❏ N
_____	_____	❏ Y ❏ N
_____	_____	❏ Y ❏ N
_____	_____	❏ Y ❏ N
_____	_____	❏ Y ❏ N
_____	_____	❏ Y ❏ N
_____	_____	❏ Y ❏ N
_____	_____	❏ Y ❏ N
_____	_____	❏ Y ❏ N
_____	_____	❏ Y ❏ N
_____	_____	❏ Y ❏ N

DEGREE_____

Date	Location	Worked?
_____	_____	❑ Y ❑ N
_____	_____	❑ Y ❑ N
_____	_____	❑ Y ❑ N
_____	_____	❑ Y ❑ N
_____	_____	❑ Y ❑ N
_____	_____	❑ Y ❑ N
_____	_____	❑ Y ❑ N
_____	_____	❑ Y ❑ N
_____	_____	❑ Y ❑ N
_____	_____	❑ Y ❑ N
_____	_____	❑ Y ❑ N
_____	_____	❑ Y ❑ N
_____	_____	❑ Y ❑ N
_____	_____	❑ Y ❑ N
_____	_____	❑ Y ❑ N
_____	_____	❑ Y ❑ N
_____	_____	❑ Y ❑ N
_____	_____	❑ Y ❑ N

DEGREE_____

Date	Location	Worked?
_____	_____	❑ Y ❑ N
_____	_____	❑ Y ❑ N
_____	_____	❑ Y ❑ N
_____	_____	❑ Y ❑ N
_____	_____	❑ Y ❑ N
_____	_____	❑ Y ❑ N
_____	_____	❑ Y ❑ N
_____	_____	❑ Y ❑ N
_____	_____	❑ Y ❑ N
_____	_____	❑ Y ❑ N
_____	_____	❑ Y ❑ N
_____	_____	❑ Y ❑ N
_____	_____	❑ Y ❑ N
_____	_____	❑ Y ❑ N
_____	_____	❑ Y ❑ N
_____	_____	❑ Y ❑ N
_____	_____	❑ Y ❑ N
_____	_____	❑ Y ❑ N

DEGREE_____

Date	Location	Worked?
_____	_____	❏ Y ❏ N
_____	_____	❏ Y ❏ N
_____	_____	❏ Y ❏ N
_____	_____	❏ Y ❏ N
_____	_____	❏ Y ❏ N
_____	_____	❏ Y ❏ N
_____	_____	❏ Y ❏ N
_____	_____	❏ Y ❏ N
_____	_____	❏ Y ❏ N
_____	_____	❏ Y ❏ N
_____	_____	❏ Y ❏ N
_____	_____	❏ Y ❏ N
_____	_____	❏ Y ❏ N
_____	_____	❏ Y ❏ N
_____	_____	❏ Y ❏ N
_____	_____	❏ Y ❏ N
_____	_____	❏ Y ❏ N
_____	_____	❏ Y ❏ N

DEGREE_____

Date	Location	Worked?
_____	_____	❑ Y ❑ N
_____	_____	❑ Y ❑ N
_____	_____	❑ Y ❑ N
_____	_____	❑ Y ❑ N
_____	_____	❑ Y ❑ N
_____	_____	❑ Y ❑ N
_____	_____	❑ Y ❑ N
_____	_____	❑ Y ❑ N
_____	_____	❑ Y ❑ N
_____	_____	❑ Y ❑ N
_____	_____	❑ Y ❑ N
_____	_____	❑ Y ❑ N
_____	_____	❑ Y ❑ N
_____	_____	❑ Y ❑ N
_____	_____	❑ Y ❑ N
_____	_____	❑ Y ❑ N
_____	_____	❑ Y ❑ N
_____	_____	❑ Y ❑ N

DEGREE_____

Date	Location	Worked?
_____	_____	❏ Y ❏ N
_____	_____	❏ Y ❏ N
_____	_____	❏ Y ❏ N
_____	_____	❏ Y ❏ N
_____	_____	❏ Y ❏ N
_____	_____	❏ Y ❏ N
_____	_____	❏ Y ❏ N
_____	_____	❏ Y ❏ N
_____	_____	❏ Y ❏ N
_____	_____	❏ Y ❏ N
_____	_____	❏ Y ❏ N
_____	_____	❏ Y ❏ N
_____	_____	❏ Y ❏ N
_____	_____	❏ Y ❏ N
_____	_____	❏ Y ❏ N
_____	_____	❏ Y ❏ N
_____	_____	❏ Y ❏ N
_____	_____	❏ Y ❏ N

DEGREE_____

Date	Location	Worked?
_____	_____	❏ Y ❏ N
_____	_____	❏ Y ❏ N
_____	_____	❏ Y ❏ N
_____	_____	❏ Y ❏ N
_____	_____	❏ Y ❏ N
_____	_____	❏ Y ❏ N
_____	_____	❏ Y ❏ N
_____	_____	❏ Y ❏ N
_____	_____	❏ Y ❏ N
_____	_____	❏ Y ❏ N
_____	_____	❏ Y ❏ N
_____	_____	❏ Y ❏ N
_____	_____	❏ Y ❏ N
_____	_____	❏ Y ❏ N
_____	_____	❏ Y ❏ N
_____	_____	❏ Y ❏ N
_____	_____	❏ Y ❏ N
_____	_____	❏ Y ❏ N

DEGREE_____

Date	Location	Worked?
_____	_____	❑ Y ❑ N
_____	_____	❑ Y ❑ N
_____	_____	❑ Y ❑ N
_____	_____	❑ Y ❑ N
_____	_____	❑ Y ❑ N
_____	_____	❑ Y ❑ N
_____	_____	❑ Y ❑ N
_____	_____	❑ Y ❑ N
_____	_____	❑ Y ❑ N
_____	_____	❑ Y ❑ N
_____	_____	❑ Y ❑ N
_____	_____	❑ Y ❑ N
_____	_____	❑ Y ❑ N
_____	_____	❑ Y ❑ N
_____	_____	❑ Y ❑ N
_____	_____	❑ Y ❑ N
_____	_____	❑ Y ❑ N
_____	_____	❑ Y ❑ N

DEGREE_____

Date	Location	Worked?
_____	_____	❏ Y ❏ N
_____	_____	❏ Y ❏ N
_____	_____	❏ Y ❏ N
_____	_____	❏ Y ❏ N
_____	_____	❏ Y ❏ N
_____	_____	❏ Y ❏ N
_____	_____	❏ Y ❏ N
_____	_____	❏ Y ❏ N
_____	_____	❏ Y ❏ N
_____	_____	❏ Y ❏ N
_____	_____	❏ Y ❏ N
_____	_____	❏ Y ❏ N
_____	_____	❏ Y ❏ N
_____	_____	❏ Y ❏ N
_____	_____	❏ Y ❏ N
_____	_____	❏ Y ❏ N
_____	_____	❏ Y ❏ N
_____	_____	❏ Y ❏ N

DEGREE_____

Date	Location	Worked?
_____	_____	❑ Y ❑ N
_____	_____	❑ Y ❑ N
_____	_____	❑ Y ❑ N
_____	_____	❑ Y ❑ N
_____	_____	❑ Y ❑ N
_____	_____	❑ Y ❑ N
_____	_____	❑ Y ❑ N
_____	_____	❑ Y ❑ N
_____	_____	❑ Y ❑ N
_____	_____	❑ Y ❑ N
_____	_____	❑ Y ❑ N
_____	_____	❑ Y ❑ N
_____	_____	❑ Y ❑ N
_____	_____	❑ Y ❑ N
_____	_____	❑ Y ❑ N
_____	_____	❑ Y ❑ N
_____	_____	❑ Y ❑ N
_____	_____	❑ Y ❑ N

DEGREE_____

Date	Location	Worked?
_____	_____	❑ Y ❑ N
_____	_____	❑ Y ❑ N
_____	_____	❑ Y ❑ N
_____	_____	❑ Y ❑ N
_____	_____	❑ Y ❑ N
_____	_____	❑ Y ❑ N
_____	_____	❑ Y ❑ N
_____	_____	❑ Y ❑ N
_____	_____	❑ Y ❑ N
_____	_____	❑ Y ❑ N
_____	_____	❑ Y ❑ N
_____	_____	❑ Y ❑ N
_____	_____	❑ Y ❑ N
_____	_____	❑ Y ❑ N
_____	_____	❑ Y ❑ N
_____	_____	❑ Y ❑ N
_____	_____	❑ Y ❑ N
_____	_____	❑ Y ❑ N

DEGREE_____

Date	Location	Worked?
_____	_____	❏ Y ❏ N
_____	_____	❏ Y ❏ N
_____	_____	❏ Y ❏ N
_____	_____	❏ Y ❏ N
_____	_____	❏ Y ❏ N
_____	_____	❏ Y ❏ N
_____	_____	❏ Y ❏ N
_____	_____	❏ Y ❏ N
_____	_____	❏ Y ❏ N
_____	_____	❏ Y ❏ N
_____	_____	❏ Y ❏ N
_____	_____	❏ Y ❏ N
_____	_____	❏ Y ❏ N
_____	_____	❏ Y ❏ N
_____	_____	❏ Y ❏ N
_____	_____	❏ Y ❏ N
_____	_____	❏ Y ❏ N
_____	_____	❏ Y ❏ N

DEGREE_____

Date	Location	Worked?
_____	_____	❏ Y ❏ N
_____	_____	❏ Y ❏ N
_____	_____	❏ Y ❏ N
_____	_____	❏ Y ❏ N
_____	_____	❏ Y ❏ N
_____	_____	❏ Y ❏ N
_____	_____	❏ Y ❏ N
_____	_____	❏ Y ❏ N
_____	_____	❏ Y ❏ N
_____	_____	❏ Y ❏ N
_____	_____	❏ Y ❏ N
_____	_____	❏ Y ❏ N
_____	_____	❏ Y ❏ N
_____	_____	❏ Y ❏ N
_____	_____	❏ Y ❏ N
_____	_____	❏ Y ❏ N
_____	_____	❏ Y ❏ N
_____	_____	❏ Y ❏ N

DEGREE_____

Date	Location	Worked?
_____	_____	❑ Y ❑ N
_____	_____	❑ Y ❑ N
_____	_____	❑ Y ❑ N
_____	_____	❑ Y ❑ N
_____	_____	❑ Y ❑ N
_____	_____	❑ Y ❑ N
_____	_____	❑ Y ❑ N
_____	_____	❑ Y ❑ N
_____	_____	❑ Y ❑ N
_____	_____	❑ Y ❑ N
_____	_____	❑ Y ❑ N
_____	_____	❑ Y ❑ N
_____	_____	❑ Y ❑ N
_____	_____	❑ Y ❑ N
_____	_____	❑ Y ❑ N
_____	_____	❑ Y ❑ N
_____	_____	❑ Y ❑ N
_____	_____	❑ Y ❑ N

DEGREE_____

Date	Location	Worked?
_____	_____	❏ Y ❏ N
_____	_____	❏ Y ❏ N
_____	_____	❏ Y ❏ N
_____	_____	❏ Y ❏ N
_____	_____	❏ Y ❏ N
_____	_____	❏ Y ❏ N
_____	_____	❏ Y ❏ N
_____	_____	❏ Y ❏ N
_____	_____	❏ Y ❏ N
_____	_____	❏ Y ❏ N
_____	_____	❏ Y ❏ N
_____	_____	❏ Y ❏ N
_____	_____	❏ Y ❏ N
_____	_____	❏ Y ❏ N
_____	_____	❏ Y ❏ N
_____	_____	❏ Y ❏ N
_____	_____	❏ Y ❏ N
_____	_____	❏ Y ❏ N

DEGREE_____

Date	Location	Worked?
_____	_____	❑ Y ❑ N
_____	_____	❑ Y ❑ N
_____	_____	❑ Y ❑ N
_____	_____	❑ Y ❑ N
_____	_____	❑ Y ❑ N
_____	_____	❑ Y ❑ N
_____	_____	❑ Y ❑ N
_____	_____	❑ Y ❑ N
_____	_____	❑ Y ❑ N
_____	_____	❑ Y ❑ N
_____	_____	❑ Y ❑ N
_____	_____	❑ Y ❑ N
_____	_____	❑ Y ❑ N
_____	_____	❑ Y ❑ N
_____	_____	❑ Y ❑ N
_____	_____	❑ Y ❑ N
_____	_____	❑ Y ❑ N
_____	_____	❑ Y ❑ N

DEGREE_____

Date	Location	Worked?
_____	_____	❏ Y ❏ N
_____	_____	❏ Y ❏ N
_____	_____	❏ Y ❏ N
_____	_____	❏ Y ❏ N
_____	_____	❏ Y ❏ N
_____	_____	❏ Y ❏ N
_____	_____	❏ Y ❏ N
_____	_____	❏ Y ❏ N
_____	_____	❏ Y ❏ N
_____	_____	❏ Y ❏ N
_____	_____	❏ Y ❏ N
_____	_____	❏ Y ❏ N
_____	_____	❏ Y ❏ N
_____	_____	❏ Y ❏ N
_____	_____	❏ Y ❏ N
_____	_____	❏ Y ❏ N
_____	_____	❏ Y ❏ N
_____	_____	❏ Y ❏ N

DEGREE_____

Date	Location	Worked?
_____	_____	❏ Y ❏ N
_____	_____	❏ Y ❏ N
_____	_____	❏ Y ❏ N
_____	_____	❏ Y ❏ N
_____	_____	❏ Y ❏ N
_____	_____	❏ Y ❏ N
_____	_____	❏ Y ❏ N
_____	_____	❏ Y ❏ N
_____	_____	❏ Y ❏ N
_____	_____	❏ Y ❏ N
_____	_____	❏ Y ❏ N
_____	_____	❏ Y ❏ N
_____	_____	❏ Y ❏ N
_____	_____	❏ Y ❏ N
_____	_____	❏ Y ❏ N
_____	_____	❏ Y ❏ N
_____	_____	❏ Y ❏ N
_____	_____	❏ Y ❏ N

DEGREE_____

Date	Location	Worked?
_____	_____	❑ Y ❑ N
_____	_____	❑ Y ❑ N
_____	_____	❑ Y ❑ N
_____	_____	❑ Y ❑ N
_____	_____	❑ Y ❑ N
_____	_____	❑ Y ❑ N
_____	_____	❑ Y ❑ N
_____	_____	❑ Y ❑ N
_____	_____	❑ Y ❑ N
_____	_____	❑ Y ❑ N
_____	_____	❑ Y ❑ N
_____	_____	❑ Y ❑ N
_____	_____	❑ Y ❑ N
_____	_____	❑ Y ❑ N
_____	_____	❑ Y ❑ N
_____	_____	❑ Y ❑ N
_____	_____	❑ Y ❑ N
_____	_____	❑ Y ❑ N

10 CHARITY WORK/CONTRIBUTIONS

In this section you may list the charity/benevolence work you have performed and/or assisted with and/or contributed to.

WORK

Date	Charity Event/Location	Amount
_____	_____	_____
_____	_____	_____
_____	_____	_____
_____	_____	_____
_____	_____	_____
_____	_____	_____
_____	_____	_____
_____	_____	_____
_____	_____	_____
_____	_____	_____
_____	_____	_____
_____	_____	_____
_____	_____	_____
_____	_____	_____
_____	_____	_____
_____	_____	_____

WORK_____

Date	Charity Event/Location	Amount
_____	_____ __	_____
_____	_____ __	_____
_____	_____ __	_____
_____	_____ __	_____
_____	_____ __	_____
_____	_____ __	_____
_____	_____ __	_____
_____	_____ __	_____
_____	_____ __	_____
_____	_____ __	_____
_____	_____ __	_____
_____	_____ __	_____
_____	_____ __	_____
_____	_____ __	_____
_____	_____ __	_____
_____	_____ __	_____
_____	_____ __	_____

WORK_____

Date	Charity Event/Location	Amount
_____	_____ --	_____
_____	_____ --	_____
_____	_____ --	_____
_____	_____ --	_____
_____	_____ --	_____
_____	_____ --	_____
_____	_____ --	_____
_____	_____ --	_____
_____	_____ --	_____
_____	_____ --	_____
_____	_____ --	_____
_____	_____ --	_____
_____	_____ --	_____
_____	_____ --	_____
_____	_____ --	_____
_____	_____ --	_____
_____	_____ --	_____

WORK_____

Date	Charity Event/Location	Amount
_____	_____ --	_____
_____	_____ --	_____
_____	_____ --	_____
_____	_____ --	_____
_____	_____ --	_____
_____	_____ --	_____
_____	_____ --	_____
_____	_____ --	_____
_____	_____ --	_____
_____	_____ --	_____
_____	_____ --	_____
_____	_____ --	_____
_____	_____ --	_____
_____	_____ --	_____
_____	_____ --	_____
_____	_____ --	_____

WORK_____

Date	Charity Event/Location	Amount
_____	_____ --	_____
_____	_____ --	_____
_____	_____ --	_____
_____	_____ --	_____
_____	_____ --	_____
_____	_____ --	_____
_____	_____ --	_____
_____	_____ --	_____
_____	_____ --	_____
_____	_____ --	_____
_____	_____ --	_____
_____	_____ --	_____
_____	_____ --	_____
_____	_____ --	_____
_____	_____ --	_____
_____	_____ --	_____

WORK_____

Date	Charity Event/Location	Amount
_____	_____	_____
_____	_____	_____
_____	_____	_____
_____	_____	_____
_____	_____	_____
_____	_____	_____
_____	_____	_____
_____	_____	_____
_____	_____	_____
_____	_____	_____
_____	_____	_____
_____	_____	_____
_____	_____	_____
_____	_____	_____
_____	_____	_____
_____	_____	_____

WORK_____

Date	Charity Event/Location	Amount
_____	_____ --	_____
_____	_____ --	_____
_____	_____ --	_____
_____	_____ --	_____
_____	_____ --	_____
_____	_____ --	_____
_____	_____ --	_____
_____	_____ --	_____
_____	_____ --	_____
_____	_____ --	_____
_____	_____ --	_____
_____	_____ --	_____
_____	_____ --	_____
_____	_____ --	_____
_____	_____ --	_____

WORK_____

Date	Charity Event/Location	Amount
_____	_____ --	_____
_____	_____ --	_____
_____	_____ --	_____
_____	_____ --	_____
_____	_____ --	_____
_____	_____ --	_____
_____	_____ --	_____
_____	_____ --	_____
_____	_____ --	_____
_____	_____ --	_____
_____	_____ --	_____
_____	_____ --	_____
_____	_____ --	_____
_____	_____ --	_____
_____	_____ --	_____
_____	_____ --	_____

WORK_____

Date	Charity Event/Location	Amount
_____	_____ --	_____
_____	_____ --	_____
_____	_____ --	_____
_____	_____ --	_____
_____	_____ --	_____
_____	_____ --	_____
_____	_____ --	_____
_____	_____ --	_____
_____	_____ --	_____
_____	_____ --	_____
_____	_____ --	_____
_____	_____ --	_____
_____	_____ --	_____
_____	_____ --	_____
_____	_____ --	_____
_____	_____ --	_____
_____	_____ --	_____

WORK_____

Date	Charity Event/Location	Amount
_____	_____ --	_____
_____	_____ --	_____
_____	_____ --	_____
_____	_____ --	_____
_____	_____ --	_____
_____	_____ --	_____
_____	_____ --	_____
_____	_____ --	_____
_____	_____ --	_____
_____	_____ --	_____
_____	_____ --	_____
_____	_____ --	_____
_____	_____ --	_____
_____	_____ --	_____
_____	_____ --	_____
_____	_____ --	_____

WORK_____

Date	Charity Event/Location	Amount
_____	_____ --	_____
_____	_____ --	_____
_____	_____ --	_____
_____	_____ --	_____
_____	_____ --	_____
_____	_____ --	_____
_____	_____ --	_____
_____	_____ --	_____
_____	_____ --	_____
_____	_____ --	_____
_____	_____ --	_____
_____	_____ --	_____
_____	_____ --	_____
_____	_____ --	_____
_____	_____ --	_____
_____	_____ --	_____

WORK_____

Date	Charity Event/Location	Amount
_____	_____ --	_____
_____	_____ --	_____
_____	_____ --	_____
_____	_____ --	_____
_____	_____ --	_____
_____	_____ --	_____
_____	_____ --	_____
_____	_____ --	_____
_____	_____ --	_____
_____	_____ --	_____
_____	_____ --	_____
_____	_____ --	_____
_____	_____ --	_____
_____	_____ --	_____
_____	_____ --	_____
_____	_____ --	_____
_____	_____ --	_____

WORK_____

Date	Charity Event/Location	Amount
_____	_____ --	_____
_____	_____ --	_____
_____	_____ --	_____
_____	_____ --	_____
_____	_____ --	_____
_____	_____ --	_____
_____	_____ --	_____
_____	_____ --	_____
_____	_____ --	_____
_____	_____ --	_____
_____	_____ --	_____
_____	_____ --	_____
_____	_____ --	_____
_____	_____ --	_____
_____	_____ --	_____
_____	_____ --	_____

WORK_____

Date	Charity Event/Location	Amount
_____	_____ --	_____
_____	_____ --	_____
_____	_____ --	_____
_____	_____ --	_____
_____	_____ --	_____
_____	_____ --	_____
_____	_____ --	_____
_____	_____ --	_____
_____	_____ --	_____
_____	_____ --	_____
_____	_____ --	_____
_____	_____ --	_____
_____	_____ --	_____
_____	_____ --	_____
_____	_____ --	_____
_____	_____ --	_____

WORK_____

Date	Charity Event/Location	Amount
_____	_____ --	_____
_____	_____ --	_____
_____	_____ --	_____
_____	_____ --	_____
_____	_____ --	_____
_____	_____ --	_____
_____	_____ --	_____
_____	_____ --	_____
_____	_____ --	_____
_____	_____ --	_____
_____	_____ --	_____
_____	_____ --	_____
_____	_____ --	_____
_____	_____ --	_____
_____	_____ --	_____
_____	_____ --	_____
_____	_____ --	_____

WORK

Date	Charity Event/Location	Amount
_____	_____ --	_____
_____	_____ --	_____
_____	_____ --	_____
_____	_____ --	_____
_____	_____ --	_____
_____	_____ --	_____
_____	_____ --	_____
_____	_____ --	_____
_____	_____ --	_____
_____	_____ --	_____
_____	_____ --	_____
_____	_____ --	_____
_____	_____ --	_____
_____	_____ --	_____
_____	_____ --	_____
_____	_____ --	_____
_____	_____ --	_____

WORK_____

Date	Charity Event/Location	Amount
_____	_____ --	_____
_____	_____ --	_____
_____	_____ --	_____
_____	_____ --	_____
_____	_____ --	_____
_____	_____ --	_____
_____	_____ --	_____
_____	_____ --	_____
_____	_____ --	_____
_____	_____ --	_____
_____	_____ --	_____
_____	_____ --	_____
_____	_____ --	_____
_____	_____ --	_____
_____	_____ --	_____
_____	_____ --	_____
_____	_____ --	_____

WORK

Date	Charity Event/Location	Amount
_____	_____ --	_____
_____	_____ --	_____
_____	_____ --	_____
_____	_____ --	_____
_____	_____ --	_____
_____	_____ --	_____
_____	_____ --	_____
_____	_____ --	_____
_____	_____ --	_____
_____	_____ --	_____
_____	_____ --	_____
_____	_____ --	_____
_____	_____ --	_____
_____	_____ --	_____
_____	_____ --	_____
_____	_____ --	_____
_____	_____ --	_____

WORK_____

Date	Charity Event/Location	Amount
_____	_____ --	_____
_____	_____ --	_____
_____	_____ --	_____
_____	_____ --	_____
_____	_____ --	_____
_____	_____ --	_____
_____	_____ --	_____
_____	_____ --	_____
_____	_____ --	_____
_____	_____ --	_____
_____	_____ --	_____
_____	_____ --	_____
_____	_____ --	_____
_____	_____ --	_____
_____	_____ --	_____
_____	_____ --	_____

11 MASONIC EDUCATION/TRAINING

In this section you may list any Masonic Education trainings, Schools of Instruction, and/or conferences you have participated in, assisted with, or contributed to.

BODY_____

Date   Training Event/Location

_____   _____   _____

_____   _____   _____

_____   _____   _____

_____   _____   _____

_____   _____   _____

_____   _____   _____

_____   _____   _____

_____   _____   _____

_____   _____   _____

_____   _____   _____

_____   _____   _____

_____   _____   _____

_____   _____   _____

_____   _____   _____

_____   _____   _____

BODY_____

Date	Training Event/Location	
_____	_____	_____
_____	_____	_____
_____	_____	_____
_____	_____	_____
_____	_____	_____
_____	_____	_____
_____	_____	_____
_____	_____	_____
_____	_____	_____
_____	_____	_____
_____	_____	_____
_____	_____	_____
_____	_____	_____
_____	_____	_____
_____	_____	_____
_____	_____	_____
_____	_____	_____
_____	_____	_____

BODY_____

Date   Training Event/Location

_____   _____ _____

_____   _____ _____

_____   _____ _____

_____   _____ _____

_____   _____ _____

_____   _____ _____

_____   _____ _____

_____   _____ _____

_____   _____ _____

_____   _____ _____

_____   _____ _____

_____   _____ _____

_____   _____ _____

_____   _____ _____

_____   _____ _____

BODY_____

Date   Training Event/Location

_____   _____   _____

_____   _____   _____

_____   _____   _____

_____   _____   _____

_____   _____   _____

_____   _____   _____

_____   _____   _____

_____   _____   _____

_____   _____   _____

_____   _____   _____

_____   _____   _____

_____   _____   _____

_____   _____   _____

_____   _____   _____

_____   _____   _____

_____   _____   _____

_____   _____   _____

BODY_____

Date   Training Event/Location

_____   _____   _____

_____   _____   _____

_____   _____   _____

_____   _____   _____

_____   _____   _____

_____   _____   _____

_____   _____   _____

_____   _____   _____

_____   _____   _____

_____   _____   _____

_____   _____   _____

_____   _____   _____

_____   _____   _____

_____   _____   _____

_____   _____   _____

BODY_____

Date   Training Event/Location

_____   _____ _____

_____   _____ _____

_____   _____ _____

_____   _____ _____

_____   _____ _____

_____   _____ _____

_____   _____ _____

_____   _____ _____

_____   _____ _____

_____   _____ _____

_____   _____ _____

_____   _____ _____

_____   _____ _____

_____   _____ _____

_____   _____ _____

_____   _____ _____

_____   _____ _____

BODY_____

Date	Training Event/Location	
_____	_____	_____
_____	_____	_____
_____	_____	_____
_____	_____	_____
_____	_____	_____
_____	_____	_____
_____	_____	_____
_____	_____	_____
_____	_____	_____
_____	_____	_____
_____	_____	_____
_____	_____	_____
_____	_____	_____
_____	_____	_____
_____	_____	_____
_____	_____	_____
_____	_____	_____
_____	_____	_____

BODY_____

Date   Training Event/Location

_____   _____ _____

_____   _____ _____

_____   _____ _____

_____   _____ _____

_____   _____ _____

_____   _____ _____

_____   _____ _____

_____   _____ _____

_____   _____ _____

_____   _____ _____

_____   _____ _____

_____   _____ _____

_____   _____ _____

_____   _____ _____

_____   _____ _____

BODY_____

Date	Training Event/Location	
_____	_____	_____
_____	_____	_____
_____	_____	_____
_____	_____	_____
_____	_____	_____
_____	_____	_____
_____	_____	_____
_____	_____	_____
_____	_____	_____
_____	_____	_____
_____	_____	_____
_____	_____	_____
_____	_____	_____
_____	_____	_____
_____	_____	_____

BODY_____

Date   Training Event/Location

BODY_____

Date   Training Event/Location

_____   _____ _____

_____   _____ _____

_____   _____ _____

_____   _____ _____

_____   _____ _____

_____   _____ _____

_____   _____ _____

_____   _____ _____

_____   _____ _____

_____   _____ _____

_____   _____ _____

_____   _____ _____

_____   _____ _____

_____   _____ _____

_____   _____ _____

_____   _____ _____

BODY_____

Date   Training Event/Location

_____   _____ _____

_____   _____ _____

_____   _____ _____

_____   _____ _____

_____   _____ _____

_____   _____ _____

_____   _____ _____

_____   _____ _____

_____   _____ _____

_____   _____ _____

_____   _____ _____

_____   _____ _____

_____   _____ _____

_____   _____ _____

_____   _____ _____

_____   _____ _____

_____   _____ _____

BODY_____

Date	Training Event/Location	
_____	_____	_____
_____	_____	_____
_____	_____	_____
_____	_____	_____
_____	_____	_____
_____	_____	_____
_____	_____	_____
_____	_____	_____
_____	_____	_____
_____	_____	_____
_____	_____	_____
_____	_____	_____
_____	_____	_____
_____	_____	_____
_____	_____	_____
_____	_____	_____

BODY_____

Date	Training Event/Location	
_____	_____	_____
_____	_____	_____
_____	_____	_____
_____	_____	_____
_____	_____	_____
_____	_____	_____
_____	_____	_____
_____	_____	_____
_____	_____	_____
_____	_____	_____
_____	_____	_____
_____	_____	_____
_____	_____	_____
_____	_____	_____
_____	_____	_____
_____	_____	_____

BODY_____

Date	Training Event/Location	
_____	_____	_____
_____	_____	_____
_____	_____	_____
_____	_____	_____
_____	_____	_____
_____	_____	_____
_____	_____	_____
_____	_____	_____
_____	_____	_____
_____	_____	_____
_____	_____	_____
_____	_____	_____
_____	_____	_____
_____	_____	_____
_____	_____	_____

BODY_____

Date	Training Event/Location	
_____	_____	_____
_____	_____	_____
_____	_____	_____
_____	_____	_____
_____	_____	_____
_____	_____	_____
_____	_____	_____
_____	_____	_____
_____	_____	_____
_____	_____	_____
_____	_____	_____
_____	_____	_____
_____	_____	_____
_____	_____	_____
_____	_____	_____
_____	_____	_____
_____	_____	_____

BODY_____

Date   Training Event/Location

_____   _____   _____

_____   _____   _____

_____   _____   _____

_____   _____   _____

_____   _____   _____

_____   _____   _____

_____   _____   _____

_____   _____   _____

_____   _____   _____

_____   _____   _____

_____   _____   _____

_____   _____   _____

_____   _____   _____

_____   _____   _____

_____   _____   _____

BODY_____

Date   Training Event/Location

BODY_____

Date   Training Event/Location

Notes

Notes

Notes

Notes

Notes

Notes

ABOUT THE AUTHOR

The Author, James F. "Chip" Hatcher III, is a Freemason and member of several regular, concordant, appendant, associated, allied, and invitational Masonic Bodies.

He lives in the foothills of the Great Smoky Mountains in Eastern Tennessee with his wife Lisa, 3 children, 3 cats, and regularly encourages other to continually seek more light through the pathways of Freemasonry.

OTHER MASONIC BOOKS
BY THE AUTHOR

at

masonicpress.com

Worshipful Master's Guidebook

The Lodge Officer's Handbook

King Solomon's Passport

Masonic Roll of Fellow Crafts

Mark Masters Lodge Book of Marks

York Rite Mason's Handbook

Scottish Rite Mason's Handbook

SO•MOTE•IT•BE

www.ingramcontent.com/pod-product-compliance
Lightning Source LLC
Chambersburg PA
CBHW060624290526
45793CB00001B/130